DATE DUE

MY 1 1 '93	JUN 27 '95	SE 28 '99	FE 15 '05
SE 27 '93	SEP 01 '95	AG 28 '00	MR 01 '05
OC 11 '93	JAN 31 '95	JA 05 '01	MR 23 '05
OC 27 '93	JL 08 '95	JA 19 '01	JY 26 '05
DEC 11 '93	AUG 20 '96	AG 09 '01	AG 27 '05
JAN 17 '94	OCT 21 '96	SE 14 '01	OC 31 '05
JUN 22 '94	JUL 31 '97	DE 08 '01	NO 03 '06
JUL 07 '94	DEC 15 '97	JY 05 '02	SE 08 '07
JUL 30 '94	JAN 20 '98	AG 09 '02	MY 05 '08
AUG 17 '94	JUN 04 '98		AG 21 '08
OCT 17 '94	OCT 20 '98	JA 29 '03	DE 12 '14
		MR 06 '03	
OCT 31 '94	FEB 11 '99	JE 14 '03	12-8-21
FEB 13 '95	AP 23 '99	MY 04 '04	12-15-22
MAR 16 '95	OC 27 '99	JA 31 '05	

OVERBOARD

An OVERBOARD Collection by Chip Dunham

Andrews and McMeel
A Universal Press Syndicate Company
Kansas City

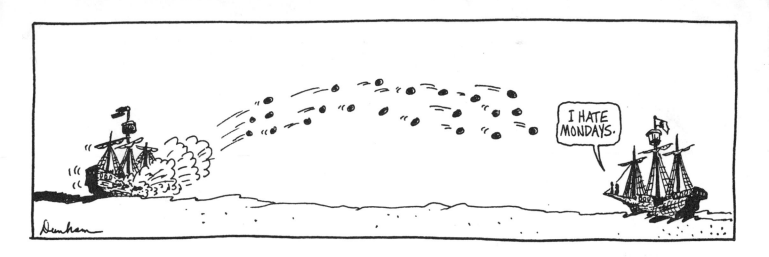

AND WHEN YOU'VE FINISHED BLOWING IT OUT OF THE WATER, BLOW THE PIECES OUT OF THE WATER;

AND WHEN YOU'RE DONE BLOWING THE PIECES OUT OF THE WATER,

THEN BLOW THE FRAGMENTS OF THE PIECES OUT OF THE WATER.

WHAT ARE WE SHOOTING AT?

THE IRS BOAT.

BOOF'S HOLDING UP A CANDLE FOR PEACE, SEAHAWK—

WHAT'S YOURS FOR?

MALE PATTERN BALDNESS RESEARCH.

Dear son, we're all fine. Your brother was just promoted to vice-president at the bank,

Your little sister is going to argue a case in front of the State Supreme Court,

and your cousin Teddy just put a big down payment on his third apartment building...

How's your scurvy?

EAU CLAIRE

ALL RIGHT. GUYS— A GOOD FENCER WILL MAKE SURE HIS HANDS ARE IN THE CORRECT POSITION,

HIS SHOULDERS ARE SQUARE, HIS HEAD ERECT,

AND HIS SABER IS AT THE CORRECT ANGLE FOR ATTACK.

WHILE HE'S THINKING ABOUT ALL THAT, SHOOT HIM.

I WOULDN'T WANT THIS SPREAD AROUND, BUT I GET PRETTY SCARED BEFORE A BATTLE, CHARLEY.

YEAH?

DON'T FEEL EMBARRASSED, MAN — LOTS OF GUYS GET A LITTLE NERVOUS BEFORE A FIGHT — AND DON'T WORRY —

I FEEL PRIVILEGED THAT YOU FELT COMFORTABLE ENOUGH WITH ME TO SHARE WHAT WAS PROBABLY A PRETTY TOUGH THING TO ADMIT.

WHAT'S UP GUYS?

BOOF'S SPILLING HIS GUTS TO ME ABOUT WHAT A LOSER CHICKEN HE IS.

YOU GUYS WANNA GO INTO TOWN AND HAVE SOME GOOD, CLEAN FUN?

I DON'T EVEN KNOW HOW TO RESPOND TO THAT ONE.

NATE, DO YOU REMEMBER LAST MONTH WHEN WE DOCKED IN THAT LITTLE PORT AND I LEASED THE CONDO?

AND I BOUGHT ALL THAT FURNITURE, HIRED SERVANTS, THREW THAT HUGE PARTY...

AND TOLD EVERYBODY HOW HAPPY I WAS IN MY NEW HOME?

YEAH?

WHAT TOWN WAS THAT?

HEY — A QUARTER!

GREAT VISION...

LOUSY DEPTH PERCEPTION.

SEE THE DIAMOND NECKLACE I TRADED A GUY FOR?

NICE, NATE — WHAT WAS THE TRADE?

HE GAVE ME THE NECKLACE AND I DIDN'T KILL HIM.

SOUNDS FAIR.

OH, YEAH. I THINK BOTH SIDES WALKED AWAY HAPPY.

HERE'S ME WALKING DOWN THE AISLE.

HERE'S MY BRIDE-TO-BE WALKING DOWN THE AISLE.

HERE'S MY BRIDE-TO-BE SMILING AT AN OLD BOYFRIEND...

THE REST ARE PRETTY MUCH WHAT THE JUDGE CALLED MY EXTREMELY VIOLENT OVERREACTION.

RED SKY AT NIGHT, SAILOR'S DELIGHT,

RED SKY AT MORNING, SAILOR TAKE WARNING.

A-WHOMP BOPPA LUBBA, A-WHOMP BAM BOOM.

OKAY, THERE'S OUR SOLEMN OATH TO REMAIN AT OUR POST AND PROTECT OUR SLEEPING COMRADES FROM THE THOUSAND PERILS OF THE SEA AT NIGHT,

AND THEN THERE'S THE CHOCOLATE CAKE IN THE FRIDGE...

WANT TO ATTACK ONE OF THOSE SHIPS, NATE?

NOT REALLY—I DON'T FEEL TOO PIRATEY TODAY.

YEAH, ME NEITHER. PLUS, I SHOULD WATER MY PLANTS.

THERE'S A CONVERSATION BLACKBEARD NEVER HAD.

WHAT DO I DO IF I GET WOUNDED?

GOOD QUESTION, BOOF—

WHAT I GENERALLY ADVISE IF YOU GET WOUNDED IS TO LOOK DOWN IN AMAZEMENT AT THE WOUND, LET YOUR SWORD CLATTER TO THE DECK, GIVE A WEAK GRIN,

AND THEN DIE.

WANT ME TO WRITE THAT DOWN FOR YOU?

WHAT ARE YOU DOING DOWN THERE, NATE?

I'M HOLDING THIS SHARK'S HEAD UNDERWATER 'TIL HE GETS REAL MAD,

THEN I'M GOING TO JUMP IN AND WRESTLE HIM.

AND THE GUY WONDERS WHY HE'S UNINSURABLE.

SO THIS IS THE NEW SELF-DESTRUCT MECHANISM, HUH?

YUP — TOTALLY VOICE-ACTIVATED.

IF WE EVER GET CAPTURED YOU JUST SAY THE SECRET PHRASE AND ONE MINUTE LATER THE WHOLE SHIP EXPLODES.

WOW.

KIND OF A RISKY THING TO HAVE AROUND, ISN'T IT?

NOT REALLY — NATE'S THE ONLY ONE WHO KNOWS THE SECRET WORDS,

AND HE WAS SUPPOSED TO PICK A PHRASE WITH ABOUT A ZERO POSSIBILITY OF BEING SAID AROUND HERE.

COOL.

WHOSE IDEA WAS THAT?

MINE.

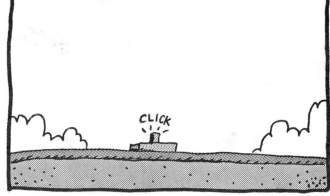

YOU'RE A SMART CAPTAIN.

CLICK

SIR? WHAT IF THERE'S LIKE, A BIG FIRE, AND YOU MIGHT HAVE CAUSED IT,

BUT YOU DEFINITELY *DON'T* WANT TO TAKE THE RAP FOR IT.

WHAT'S THE PROCEDURE?

HYPOTHETICALLY, I MEAN.

THE CAPTAIN SURE LOOKS LOST IN THOUGHT UP THERE.

WELL, LOOK AT THE DEMANDS OF THE JOB, BOOF...

COMING UP WITH BATTLE PLANS, FORMULATING LONG- AND SHORT-TERM STRATEGY...

THE GUY'S GOT A LOT ON HIS MIND.

THERE'S A PRETTY WAVE... THERE'S A PRETTY WAVE... THERE'S A PRETTY WAVE...

A BLACK BUTTERFLY!! WATCH OUT! IF IT LANDS ON YOU IT'S A SIGN OF **IMMINENT DEATH!!**

SCRAM! SCAT! GET OUTTA HERE!!

OKAY, IT'S GONE. KEEP YOUR EYES PEELED, THOUGH...

LOTS OF TIMES THEY TRAVEL IN PAIRS.

31

34

SO COME ON — IF YOU WERE AN EDITOR HOW WOULD YOU REACT TO MY MANUSCRIPT?

BUT HEY — THAT'S JUST ONE OPINION...

WE QUIT!

GOOD!

NICE CONTRACT PLOY, CHARLEY.

HOW DO THE BOYS LIKE THE NEW POOL TABLE, NATE?

WELL, THEY PLAYED A FEW GAMES ON IT, GOT INTO A BIG ARGUMENT, BROKE ALL THE CUESTICKS OVER EACH OTHER'S HEADS,

THEN THEY DRAGGED THE TABLE OUT ON DECK, SET IT ON FIRE, AND PUSHED THE WHOLE THING OVERBOARD.

I KNEW THEY'D GET A KICK OUT OF IT.

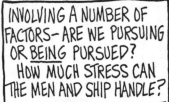

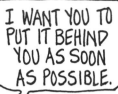

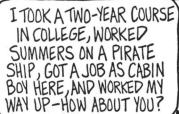

BOOF, I'LL BET A LOT OF PEOPLE MISTAKE YOUR QUIET DEMEANOR FOR STUPIDITY.

I KNOW I DO.

HEY GUYS — THAT TOP STEP GOING DOWN TO THE GALLEY IS ROTTED OUT. IF ANYONE TAKES A FALL ON IT THEY'RE GONNA BREAK THEIR NECK.

SO PASS THE WORD, OKAY?

OKAY.

FRESH BROWNIES, SIR.

FROM THE CAPTAIN: I'VE NOTICED LATELY THAT WHEN WE BOARD ENEMY SHIPS, SOME OF YOU HAVE NOT BEEN LEAPING EFFORTLESSLY.

LEAPING EFFORTLESSLY IS AS IMPORTANT TO OUR PUBLIC IMAGE AS A GOOD PIRATE GRIN.

IN THE FUTURE PLEASE TRY TO LEAP EFFORTLESSLY.

KEEP A COPY OF THAT FOR HIS EVENTUAL SANITY HEARING.

I WANT THAT BLUE SHIP STRIPPED OF EVERYTHING VALUABLE, NATE.

I WANT THEIR CASH AND JEWELS BROUGHT ON BOARD,

I WANT THE SHIP SET ON FIRE,

THE CREW DUMPED INTO A LEAKY, TWO-DOLLAR ROWBOAT,

AND THEN I WANT MEAT THROWN ALL AROUND IT TO ATTRACT HUGE MAN-EATING SHARKS, OKAY?

OKAY.

THE GUY IS ROUGH ON TAILGATERS.

HEY, CHARLEY AND SEAHAWK— YOUR OLD HIGH SCHOOL IN TOWN BLEW UP LAST NIGHT.

"NO ONE WAS INJURED IN THE BLAST, BUT ENOUGH DYNAMITE WAS USED TO BLOW THE BUILDING SIX HUNDRED FEET IN THE AIR."

I'LL LEAVE THIS IN THE LUNCHROOM SO YOU CAN READ IT LATER.

WHAT WAS HE SAYING?

WHO KNOWS? MY EARS ARE STILL RINGING LIKE CRAZY.

ANYBODY SEEN MY BRAND-NEW LITTLE PORTABLE TV?

WELL, ALL I CAN SAY IS IT'S NOT IN MY ROOM.

I ONLY HAVE A FEW THINGS IN MY ROOM, BUT ALL THE STUFF IN MY ROOM IS MINE.

SO ALL I CAN DO IS TELL YOU WHAT IS AND ISN'T IN MY ROOM—AND YOUR TV IS NOT IN MY ROOM.

HOPE HE DOESN'T LOOK IN MY ROOM...

WHY'S EVERYBODY RUNNING, SEAHAWK?

CHARLEY'S THROWING POISON DARTS IN THE LUNCHROOM!

HEY—I HANDLED THE JELLO FIGHT.

HOW DO YOU THINK WE'LL DO IN THE BATTLE TOMORROW, SEAHAWK?

WELL, WE'RE EVENLY MATCHED IN MEN, SAME KIND OF CANNON, SAME SIZE SHIP—

ABOUT THE ONLY DIFFERENCE IS THEY DON'T HAVE A BUMBLING, CEMENT-HEAD IDIOT RUNNING THE SHOW.

DID I SAY THAT LAST PART OUT LOUD?

LET'S SEE... OVER THERE I COULD GET HURT...

BUT OVER HERE I CAN'T GET HURT.

I THINK,

THEREFORE I STILL AM...

AND THEN I SHOWED HER THE TRICK WHERE I SPREAD THE WHITE PAPER ON THE FLOOR, JUMP UP AND DOWN REAL HARD, AND ALL THE FLEAS COME OUT.

I LOVE LISTENING TO YOU TRY AND FIGURE OUT WHY YOU NEVER GET A SECOND DATE.

CANNONBALLS ALL OVER THE PLACE...

TORN SAILS AND SHATTERED MASTS...

TOTAL DESTRUCTION, SEVENTEEN GUYS MISSING...

THIS WAS OUR BEST COMPANY PICNIC EVER.

THIS IS REALLY A WIDE LAKE.

RIVER.

OCEAN — THIS IS REALLY A WIDE OCEAN.

OH SURE — RUN AND TELL EVERYBODY.

PIRATING IS WEIRD...

I GOT A POCKETFUL OF DIAMONDS BUT I'M STANDING IN THE RAIN.

YOU'VE GOT TO SEND THAT ONE TO RANDY TRAVIS.

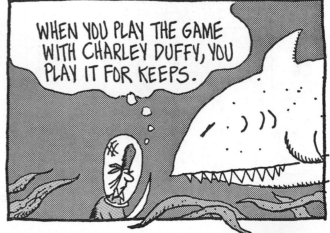

OTHER THAN THE FACT THAT WHALES DON'T LOOK LIKE THAT,

AND THE SUN IS WAY-WAY-WAY OUT OF PROPORTION,

THIS IS BETTER THAN MOST OF THE SLOP YOU COME UP WITH...

I LIKE THE NUDE ON THE JET-SKI.

YOU READY, GUYS? WE'RE GONNA RACE UP TO THAT ENEMY SHIP, MAKE THREATENING GESTURES—

WAVE OUR SWORDS AROUND — AND SAIL AWAY!

HOW TO STAY OUT OF THE PIRATE HALL OF FAME.

OKAY, I MISSED A FEW SHIPS—

AND THE CAPTAIN'S GOT A PERFECT RIGHT TO QUESTION MY EYESIGHT—

BUT I RESENT THIS FEELING THAT I'M CONSTANTLY BEING TESTED NOW.

KNOW WHAT I MEAN?

 I HAVE TO TAKE BACK A LOT OF THE MEAN THINGS I'VE SAID ABOUT CHARLEY AND SEAHAWK.

YEAH?

 YEAH—FIRST OF ALL, I DIDN'T EVEN THINK THEY'D SHOW UP FOR BOOF'S BIRTHDAY PARTY—

 AND THEN NOT ONLY DO THEY SHOW UP—

 BUT THEY BRING HIM A NICE, BIG PIÑATA!!

 I KNOW WHAT YOU MEAN— IT'S NICE TO SEE 'EM JOIN THE FUN AND CONTRIBUTE TO THE PARTY ATMOSPHERE.

 IT REALLY IS—SO LET'S CROWD IN FOR THE BIG FINALE, HUH?

 STAY ON YOUR TOES, CHARLEY—

 CUZ THOSE WASPS ARE GONNA COME OUT OF THERE MAD.

OKAY, MEN, WE'RE VASTLY OUTNUMBERED, THEY HAVE TWICE AS MANY CANNON AS WE DO, A LOT OF YOU AREN'T GONNA MAKE IT BACK—

AND THE FUNNY THING IS — I DON'T EVEN THINK THERE'S A LOT OF TREASURE OVER THERE.

THANK YOU, KNUTE ROCKNE...

SOME OF THE GUYS WERE JUST SAYING THAT YOU STINK AS A CAPTAIN.

I COULDN'T BELIEVE IT! THEY WERE JUST STANDING THERE SAYING THAT YOU STINK AS A CAPTAIN. I FELT SO...

...WHAT'S THE WORD...

CONNECTED TO EVERYONE..

I CAN'T BELIEVE IT!! YOU GUYS WENT OVER TO ATTACK THE CRUISE SHIP AND YOU WOUND UP MAKING FRIENDS?!!

YOU GUYS ARE PIRATES! YOU ATTACK AND ROB! YOU DO NOT BUDDY UP TO POTENTIAL VICTIMS, OKAY?!

OKAY.

HI, SIR—

CHARLEY SHOW YOU HIS TROPHY FROM THE LIMBO CONTEST?

WE'RE LOST! WE HAVE NO IDEA WHERE WE ARE— AND IT'S ALL YOU GUYS' FAULT!!

SLAM!!

I REALLY HATE THIS.

GETTING YELLED AT?

NAH..

WAITING 'TIL HE'S ALL THE WAY DOWN THE HALL BEFORE WE START GIGGLING.

RED ALERT!! RED ALERT!! CODE BLUE! CODE BLUE!!

WOW—THERE WAS A SENSE OF REAL URGENCY ABOUT THAT.

REALLY.

ANYWAY, MY SECOND SHOT LANDS ABOUT EIGHT FEET OFF THE GREEN, RIGHT?

ARE WE GONNA MAKE TOWN TONIGHT, SIR?

I DON'T THINK SO, GUYS—

NOT UNLESS WE LIGHTEN THE LOAD AND DUMP SOME JUNK.

NO, MAN— IF YOU WANNA SEE THE REALLY PRETTY FISH YOU GOTTA LEAN WAY OVER.

THERE'S KIND OF A POETIC IMAGE FOR YA, HUH, NATE? THE LOVELY AND FRAGILE BUTTERFLY—

JUXTAPOSED WITH THE UGLY, GROSS, NEARLY SUBHUMAN CRIMINAL?

I HEARD IT, TOO— SORT OF A MUFFLED SCREAM AND THEN A SPLASH, RIGHT?

YOU KNOW, WITH ALL THIS TALK ABOUT THE BERMUDA TRIANGLE, LET ME ASK YOU SOMETHING—

IN ALL THE YEARS WE'VE SAILED IT—

YOU EVER SEEN ANYTHING YOU COULD REALLY POINT AT AND SAY "NOW THAT'S WEIRD"?

I'M GONNA WAKE YOU GUYS UP PRETTY EARLY TOMORROW, OKAY?—

WE'RE GONNA PUT BROKEN GLASS ALL AROUND THE DECK AND DO SOME KICKBOXING TO TOUGHEN UP OUR FEET.

GREAT—

WHICH REMINDS ME— YOU GOT A QUARTER, NATE?

HITMEN... HITMEN... NOPE—

TRY "CONTRACT KILLERS."

73

YOU'VE HAD SIXTEEN PARTNERS IN THE LAST TEN MONTHS AND THEY'VE ALL PLUNGED ACCIDENTALLY TO THEIR DEATHS?

YEAH-I KNOW IT SOUNDS FISHY-

BUT SOMEWHERE AROUND HERE I GOT A REPORT ABSOLVING ME OF ALL BLAME IN THE MATTER..

YEAH-HERE IT IS..

WANNA CHECK IT OUT?

THIS IS THE ONE YOU'RE ENTERING IN THE ART SHOW, HUH?

YEAH-I JUST GOTTA THINK OF A TITLE..

HOW ABOUT "DEATH OF A CANVAS"?

I DON'T KNOW IF YOU'VE NOTICED, BUT THERE'S A SADNESS IN MY EYES EVEN WHEN I'M LAUGHING AT ONE OF YOUR FUNNY REMARKS.

I GUESS I'VE SEEN SO MUCH PAIN, SO MUCH SORROW, THAT A LITTLE SADNESS INVADES EVEN MY HAPPIEST MOMENTS.

ARE YOU BUYING ANY OF THIS?

SIR! BOOF JUST GOT BITTEN BY A POISONOUS SNAKE — WHERE'S THE SNAKE KIT?!

SNAKE KIT.. SNAKE KIT..

PROBABLY AT THE SNAKE KIT STORE, HUH?

THIS COULD BE PRETTY AWKWARD, HUH? — DOING JOB EVALUATIONS ON EACH OTHER? —

LUCKILY, WE'RE SUCH GOOD BUDDIES THAT WE'LL OVERLOOK ANY FAULTS AND GIVE EACH OTHER GLOWING RECOMMENDATIONS.

OKAY, I'M SENSING SOMETHING HERE...

YES, AND I'LL GIVE IT ALL BACK ... YES, AND I'LL GIVE IT ALL BACK... YES, AND I'LL GIVE IT ALL BACK..

CHARLEY — DID YOU BREAK INTO MY WALL SAFE?!

NO — I DIDN'T EVEN KNOW YOU HAD ONE.

MAN — EVEN WHEN I PRACTICE...

AND THEN ONE DAY SHE JUST LOOKED AT ME AND SAID, "I DON'T LOVE YOU ANYMORE."

WOW..

YOU WONDER WHAT HAPPENS TO SOME PEOPLE...

DO THEY JUST WAKE UP A LITTLE SMARTER ONE DAY, YA THINK?..

WATCHA DOING, CHARLEY?

WATCHING NATE BEING SLOWLY, SILENTLY STRANGLED BY A SLEAZY, SLIMY SEASNAKE.

WOW..

SAY THAT THREE TIMES FAST, HEY?

HEY, NATE—GOT ANY ADVICE FOR SOMEONE WHO HASN'T GONE ON A LOT OF THESE RAIDS?

SURE, BOOF.

TAKE TWO SWORDS AND HACK AT ANYTHING THAT MOVES.

OKAY— HOW ABOUT FOR SOMEONE WHO'S SANE?

YOU KNOW WHY I'M PUTTING YOU RIGHT UP FRONT FOR THIS BATTLE, BOOF?—

I'M PUTTING YOU UP FRONT BECAUSE I NEED A FIGHTING MACHINE ON THIS SPOT.

WHEN THOSE ENEMY PIRATES COME SWARMING OVER THE DECK I NEED A WARRIOR HERE—

A BATTLER!

AND THAT BATTLER IS YOU, BOOF. YOU'VE GOT THE COURAGE, THE NERVES OF STEEL..

AND THE RAW FIGHTING ABILITY TO DEFEND THIS SHIP AGAINST ANY PIRATES CRAZY ENOUGH TO GET IN YOUR WAY.

BUT WHADDYA SAY WE TAKE A QUICK SECOND HERE AND TALK A LITTLE BIT ABOUT IMAGE?

A QUIET SNEER PLAYS ACROSS SEAHAWK DUFFY'S FACE..

THEY CANNOT BEND HIM— THEY CANNOT BREAK HIM. HE IS STONE.. HE IS STEEL—

AND HE CANNOT BE MOVED..

I DON'T CARE HOW LONG YOU SIT THERE, SEAHAWK— YOU'RE GONNA EAT THOSE PEAS..

I HAVE A HUGE HEADACHE TODAY, FELLAS, SO I'D APPRECIATE A LITTLE QUIET..

IN FACT, I'D APPRECIATE A LOT OF QUIET, OKAY?

SURE.

NO PROBLEM.

I LOVE IT WHEN A DAY SUDDENLY HAS PURPOSE.

THERE'S BATTERIES IN THE AIRHORN, RIGHT?

BOY, CHARLEY—SOMETIMES IT SEEMS LIKE PEOPLE AROUND HERE JUST LOOK FOR ANY OPPORTUNITY TO START A FIGHT.

YEAH—

I KNOW EXACTLY WHAT YOU MEAN..

CREEP..

STAND ON THE ROCK AND WE'LL BE RIGHT BACK...

JUST STAND ON THE ROCK AND WE'LL BE RIGHT BACK.

THIS KIND OF STUFF HAPPENED TO ME A LOT IN HIGH SCHOOL, TOO...

YOU KNOW HOW, WHEN WE SINK A SHIP, PEOPLE SCRAMBLE TO GET INTO THE LIFEBOATS,

AND THEY'RE ALL MAD AND TRYING TO STAND UP AND SHAKE THEIR FISTS AT US?

YEAH?

WE GOTTA GET THE CAMCORDER FIXED.

HOW'D THE BRAIN SURGERY GO, SEAHAWK?

WELL, THEY HAD TO SNIP A LOT OF MEMORY AND IDENTITY NERVES,

BUT I GUESS IT WENT OKAY.

GOOD—GLAD TO HEAR IT.

SOME-THING ELSE?

YEAH—ARE WE HORSES?

"FROM THE CAPTAIN: DEAR CHARLEY AND SEAHAWK, THANKS FOR HELPING ME TEST MY NEW INVENTION, THE SEARCH-O-MATIC."

"YOU'RE A BRAVE PAIR TO RISK YOUR VERY LIVES ON SOMETHING THAT'S STILL IN THE DEVELOPMENT STAGE."

"I FIRMLY BELIEVE, THOUGH, THAT WHEN YOU TURN IT ON, THE SEARCH-O-MATIC'S STRONG LASER BEAM WILL GUIDE US THROUGH THE MOUNTAINOUS WAVES TO YOUR RESCUE..."

"AND SINCE THAT'S THE ONLY WAY WE'LL EVER FIND THAT TINY ROCK AGAIN, I CERTAINLY HOPE WE GOT ALL THE LITTLE DESIGN GLITCHES WORKED OUT."

"P.S.: NATE'S STILL CONCERNED ABOUT THE ON-SWITCH BEING THE SAME COLOR AS THE BATTERY EJECT—"

"YOU GUYS HAVE ANY THOUGHTS ON THAT?"

ISN'T IT KIND OF DANGEROUS ANCHORING A PIRATE SHIP SO CLOSE TO THE CITY?

IT DEFINITELY IS..

BUT TO ME IT'S WORTH THE RISK TO LET THE GUYS GET OFF THE SHIP ONCE IN A WHILE.

THE CITY OFFERS SO MANY THINGS WE DON'T HAVE ON BOARD, NATE— MUSEUMS, THE THEATER, FINE DINING — AND WHILE I KNOW THEY'RE NOT REALLY INTO THAT STUFF...

I THINK IT'S IMPORTANT THAT THEY GET A CHANCE TO SAMPLE IT — SO YEAH, THIS IS RISKY—

BUT IT'S HELPING THE GUYS SPREAD THEIR INTELLECTUAL WINGS..

..SO IT'S A RISK I'M HAPPY TO TAKE.

MORE HEADLIGHTS.

OKAY— WHO NEEDS AN EGG?

SOMEBODY JUST CALLED— I DIDN'T GET THE NAME— SAID IT WAS A MATTER OF LIFE OR DEATH THAT YOU GET BACK TO 'EM RIGHT AWAY..

AND THE NUMBER STARTED WITH EIGHT—

I THINK.

WHAT— NO TIP?

YOU MISERABLE PIGS..

YOU STINKING, MISERABLE, GOOD-FOR-NOTHING PIGS..

GEEZ, CHARLEY..

I DON'T THINK MOM LIKES THE NURSING HOME..

NO, HE'S NOT WORRIED, DOC..

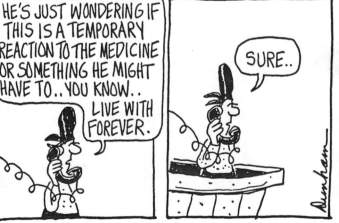

HE'S JUST WONDERING IF THIS IS A TEMPORARY REACTION TO THE MEDICINE OR SOMETHING HE MIGHT HAVE TO.. YOU KNOW.. LIVE WITH FOREVER.

SURE..

HE'S CHECKING.

HEY NATE - YOU'RE GOING OVER TO OUR FORMER FRIENDS BUT NOW BITTER ENEMY, THE GREEN SHIP?

YEAH.

AND YOU'RE GONNA SMASH AND GRAB EVERYTHING IN SIGHT..

LEAVING THEM DAZED, CONFUSED, AND SORRY THEY EVER EVEN HEARD OF US?

YEAH.

GET MY BAKING DISH, TOO..

HEY, IT'S NOT THAT I'M AGAINST CHANGE, NATE - BUT IF WE'RE GONNA GO ON A PIRATE RAID, COME ON..

LET'S SHOW AT LEAST A LITTLE RESPECT FOR TRADITION, OKAY?

YEAH-SORRY..

GUYS?

HOW ARE THEY DOING UP THERE?

WELL, CROW'S NEST IS A DELICATE JOB, NATE— BEING COOPED UP WITH THE SAME GUY ALL DAY..

BUT I HAVE A PRETTY GOOD FEEL FOR THESE THINGS - CALL IT A SIXTH SENSE..

AND I THINK WE FINALLY GOT A PAIR UP THERE THAT'LL WORK TOGETHER FOR A GOOD, LONG TIME.

COME ON... ONE MORE TIME WITH THE IRRITATING LITTLE COUGH..

SIR? COULD I ASK YOU A HUGE FAVOR?

I WONDER IF YOU'D LET ME TAKE YOUR BEAUTIFUL JEWEL-ENCRUSTED SABER DOWNSTAIRS TO SHOW THE OTHER GUYS?

Dunham

WE WERE JUST TALKING ABOUT IT—AND SOME OF THEM HAVE NEVER EVEN SEEN IT.

WHY SURE, CHARLEY— TAKE IT RIGHT OUT OF THE DISPLAY CASE.

GARBAGE DISPOSAL'S REALLY JAMMED UP, HUH?

YEAH— CHARLEY'S UP LOOKING FOR A STICK OR SOMETHING TO POKE AROUND IN THERE WITH.

CHARLEY, ARE YOU GONNA BAKE ONE OF YOUR NEAT CAKES FOR MY BIRTHDAY?

WELL, AT FIRST I WASN'T—

BUT THEN I THOUGHT "WHAT A GREAT OPPORTUNITY TO SLIP SOMETHING GROSS AND DISGUSTING INTO THE BATTER THAT YOU'D EAT WITHOUT EVEN KNOWING.."

SO HECK, YEAH, I'M BAKING YOU A CAKE!

HOW COME WE'VE NEVER JUST KILLED HIM?

HIS MOM SENDS THE BEST FOOD PACKAGES.

Dunham

AND SO, ON THIS, YOUR BIRTHDAY, WE PRESENT YOU WITH THIS TESTIMONIAL SCROLL, WHICH CELEBRATES YOUR COURAGE, YOUR LEADERSHIP..

AND ALL THE HARD WORK YOU'VE DONE EVEN THOUGH WE'RE STILL A LAUGHINGSTOCK THAT ALL THE OTHER SHIPS BEAT UP ON FOR EASY VICTORIES.

THAT LAST PART PROBABLY WOULD HAVE SOUNDED BETTER IN LATIN, HUH?

Dunham

WHAT'S GOING ON, NATE? — WHY THE SUDDEN HALT?

I'M NOT REALLY SURE—

CHARLEY AND SEAHAWK CAME RUNNING IN HERE YELLING, "SLAM ON THE BRAKES!! SLAM ON THE BRAKES!!"—THEN THEY GRABBED THEIR DIVING GEAR AND JUMPED OVERBOARD.

WHATEVER'S GOING ON, THEY WERE VERY UPSET.

YEAH? YOU WANT UPSET?

WE WERE ABOUT TWO MINUTES AWAY FROM CATCHING THE BIGGEST CRUISE SHIP I'VE SEEN IN A YEAR — THAT'S UPSET!

ALL I CAN DO NOW IS HOPE WHATEVER THE HECK THEY'RE AFTER DOWN THERE WILL SOMEHOW MAKE UP FOR IT.

BOY, SEAHAWK—IS THIS OUR LUCKY DAY OR WHAT?

THE SANDWICHES ARE ONLY SLIGHTLY DAMP AND BOTH TWINKIES ARE FINE..

YOU KNOW WHY I TOLERATE ALL THE DIRTY TRICKS YOU GUYS PLAY?—

I TOLERATE 'EM BECAUSE IF IT EVER COMES DOWN TO A REAL BATTLE, MY INTUITION TELLS ME YOU GUYS'LL BE RIGHT THERE BACKING ME UP WITH ALL YOUR SKILL AND COURAGE.

Dunham

WOW..

HOW'D YOU LIKE TO BE WALKING AROUND WITH INTUITION LIKE THAT?

HEY, HAVE YOU SEEN MY TROPHY FOR "BEST CROW'S NEST GUY"?

YEAH—

I PRIED THE DIAMOND OUT OF IT, BEAT IT INTO A SHAPELESS MASS WITH A HAMMER..

AND THREW IT DOWN IN THE HOLD WHERE ALL THE SLUDGE COLLECTS.

OH—YOU WANTED IT?

Dunham

LET ME SEE IF I GOT THIS STRAIGHT, SEAHAWK—WE'RE NOT GONNA ROB THIS PLACE?

NOPE.

WE'RE NOT GONNA TEAR SINKS OFF THE WALL OR BUG PEOPLE? WE'RE JUST GONNA WATCH THE MOVIE?

YUP.

Dunham

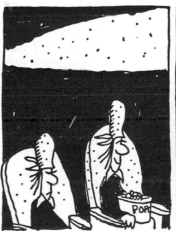

I REALLY WISH YOU'D HAVE TOLD ME THIS BEFORE I ROWED ALL THE WAY INTO TOWN.

GOSH, I DIDN'T KNOW THERE WAS ALL THIS RITUAL INVOLVED WHEN THE CAPTAIN FIGHTS A SWORD DUEL.

OH YEAH—

HE LIKES THESE THINGS CONDUCTED WITH A GREAT DEAL OF CEREMONY—

THE FIRST THING HE'LL DO IS WELCOME THE ENEMY CAPTAIN WITH A DEEP, GRACEFUL BOW...

NEXT, HE'LL RAISE HIS JEWELED SWORD IN A GESTURE OF RESPECT FOR HIS OPPONENT'S SKILLS..

AND THEN—

WHEN THE ENEMY CAPTAIN IS STANDING ON HIS EXACT MARK—

OUR CAPTAIN WILL LOOK HIM STRAIGHT IN THE EYE AND SAY, "DEFEND THYSELF OH VALIANT FOE..."

THAT'S OUR SIGNAL.

Dunham

EVEN THOUGH IT WOULD <u>WRECK</u> MY TOUGH-GUY IMAGE TO BE SEEN DOING THIS..

SOMETIMES I JUST GOTTA <u>DANCE</u>!!

BUT I'M <u>CAGEY</u> ABOUT IT—AND I ONLY DO IT IN THE EARLY, EARLY MORNING WHEN EVERYONE'S STILL <u>ASLEEP</u>!

THAT WAY THERE'S <u>NO ONE</u> TO MAKE FUN..

MY REPUTATION AS A TOUGH GUY STAYS <u>SAFE</u> AND <u>SECURE</u>..

AND MY HEART IS <u>FREE</u> TO <u>LEAP</u>..

TO FROLIC..

TO DANCE!

IS THIS GONNA BE A HIT AT THE PIRATE BANQUET OR <u>WHAT</u>?

REALLY—CAN YOU ZOOM IN ON THAT BIG SPLIT HE JUST PUT IN HIS PANTS?

SO I SMASHED HIM, THEN HE SMASHED ME BACK, SO I DOUBLE-SMASHED HIM, WHICH LEFT ME ABOUT THE ONLY ONE STILL CONSCIOUS..

SO I JUST ATTACHED SOME DYNAMITE TO THEIR HULL AND SWAM BACK OVER HERE.

UH-HUH.

I DON'T KNOW WHAT MADE ME THINK NATE'D BE A GOOD GUY TO SEND TO THE PEACE TALKS..

DO YOU KNOW WHAT HAPPENED TO MY BIG BAG OF GOLD COINS, NATE?

YEAH, CHARLEY..

I'M BIGGER THAN YOU, AND STRONGER THAN YOU, SO I PUT IT IN MY ROOM.

I CAN'T SAY I'M REAL CRAZY ABOUT HIS THEORY OF OWNERSHIP...

HELP ME, CHARLEY—I'VE BEEN STARING AT THAT PRETTY GIRL ON THE DOCK FOR AN HOUR—SHE'S SO LOVELY, SMART-LOOKING AND SOPHISTICATED..

HOW CAN I GET HER TO NOTICE ME? HOW CAN I LET HER KNOW I EVEN EXIST?

HAVE YOU TRIED THIS?

YO! BABY! YEAH YOU! MY FRIEND THE BIG APE HERE LIKES YOUR LEGS!

WELL, I DEFINITELY EXIST..

HEY, NO CHARGE—MY QUESTION IS—DO YOU REALLY WANNA HANG OUT WITH SOMEONE WHO LOOKS AT YOU WITH ALL THAT SCORN?

HEY—THANKS FOR MAILING MY LETTER.

NO PROBLEM, CHARLEY.

I WAS JUST THINKING HOW IRONIC THAT WAS—YOU MAILING MY LETTER TO THE PIRATE COUNCIL TELLING WHAT A JOKE YOU ARE AS A CAPTAIN.

HE DISAPPEARS IN THE NEXT STORM, OKAY?

SIR! STORM CLOUDS THE COLOR OF LIZ TAYLOR'S EYES WHEN THEY'RE FLASHING ANGRILY AT A REPORTER OFF THE STARBOARD BOW, SIR!

WOULD IT KILL ONE OF THESE GUYS TO ACTUALLY SAY SOMETHING PIRATEY ONCE IN AWHILE?

I'M LOOKING FOR TWO VOLUNTEERS FOR A HIGHLY DANGEROUS MISSION.

IF THIS IS GONNA BE A STARING CONTEST, YOU'RE GONNA NEED A CHAIR, OKAY?

MAN, CHARLEY—THIS RIGHT FIELD IS SOME DEEP GRASS.

YEAH—THANKS FOR SWITCHING WITH ME, SEAHAWK.

ANY TIPS FOR ME?

YEAH—IT'S A LITTLE TOUGHER TO KEEP YOUR EYE ON THE BALL IN THERE..

AND THE GREEN LOG IS A CROCODILE.

LOOK, BOOF—THE GREEN SHIP GUYS ARE THE HOME TEAM—SO THEY GOT TO PICK THE BALLFIELD..

THIS IS NOT A WELL-GROOMED PARK, AND OBVIOUSLY THE CONDITIONS AREN'T IDEAL— BUT WE'RE GONNA HAVE TO DEAL WITH THAT, OKAY?

OKAY.

AND WHEN SOME DUMB LITTLE THING HAPPENS, WHAT ARE WE GONNA DO?

WE'RE GONNA FORGET ABOUT IT AND KEEP PLAYING

'ATTA BOY. WE'LL GET A LITTLE ICE ON THAT PUNCTURE WOUND WHEN YOU COME IN TO BAT.

I COULD CATCH THIS FLY BALL..

WITH MY HAND-EYE COORDINATION AND OVERALL ATHLETIC SKILL IT'D BE A SNAP CATCHING THIS FLY BALL..

BUT ATTENTION SPAN..

I COULD REALLY USE A LITTLE WORK ON ATTENTION SPAN..

YOU KNOW WHY I'M EXCITED ABOUT THIS RACE FOR PIRATE COUNCIL, NATE?

WHY?

'CUZ I THINK YOU AND I CAN RUN AGAINST EACH OTHER WITHOUT ALL THOSE DIRTY TRICKS CANDIDATES ARE ALWAYS PULLING.

WELL, CHARLEY, I'M WILLING IF YOU ARE.

REALLY? BECAUSE IF YOU MEAN THAT, THEN I'M GLAD WE BUMPED INTO EACH OTHER—

NOW WE CAN TURN OUR FULL ATTENTION TO THE ISSUES, RUN A FAIR AND SQUARE CAMPAIGN..

AND GIVE THIS SHIP THE BEST DARN ELECTION RACE IT'S SEEN IN YEARS!

GREAT.

VOTE

I'D LIKE TO START OUT BY SAYING I JUST HAD A VERY NICE CHAT WITH—

BLAM!!

WHERE'S MY "STUNNED BY THIS TRAGIC AND UN-FORESEEN EVENT" SPEECH, SEAHAWK?

SHOULD BE RIGHT UNDER THE DYNAMITE RECEIPT..

Dunham

YOU HURT YOUR ANKLE AGAIN, NATE?

YEAH.

IT HURTS TOO MUCH TO PLAY?

YEAH.

BUT YOU STILL WANT TO HELP THE TEAM?

SURE.

DO YOU KNOW WHAT "POM-POMS" ARE?

SEAHAWK, I THINK YOU HANDLED OUR DEFEAT IN TODAY'S BALL GAME WITH THE GREEN SHIP VERY WELL.

THANK YOU.

YOU TOOK THE LOSS LIKE A TRUE GENTLEMAN, AND YOU DISPLAYED REAL SPORTSMANSHIP.

THANKS.

SOME OF US COULD LEARN A THING OR TWO FROM YOUR EXAMPLE..

I will not blow up expensive opposing teams' buses..
I will not blow up expensive opposing teams' buses..

ME AND SEAHAWK LEARNED SOMETHING ABOUT OURSELVES TODAY.

YEAH?

WE CAN HIDE IN THE BROOM CLOSET DURING A BATTLE AND NOT LOSE OUR SENSE OF DIGNITY AS PIRATES OR MEN.

I'M CERTAINLY CLICKING MY HEELS..

CHARLEY, GO TELL NATE TO START DRIFTING TOWARD THAT HEAVILY ARMED ENEMY SHIP.

TOWARD?

YEAH, TOWARD.

TOWARD?

YES— TOWARD.

IT'S FUNNY— YOU KEEP SAYING "TOWARD"...

HOW DOES YOUR NOSE FEEL, SIR?

MY NOSE? FINE.

IT DOESN'T FEEL WEIRD, LIKE IT'S GOING TO ROT OR DROP RIGHT OFF?

NO.

LAST TIME I SPEND EIGHTY BUCKS ON A GYPSY CURSE...

SEE HIM OVER THERE? THE GRAY RAT DRAGGING THE HAMBONE INTO THAT CRACK IN THE WALL?

THE SNARLING ONE WITH THE RABIES FOAM IN THE CORNERS OF HIS MOUTH?

YEAH—

CAN I KEEP HIM?

BOOF'S STILL PRETTY SHOOK UP BY HIS CLOSE CALL WITH THE SHARK, HUH?

YEAH, HE'S TOTALLY TRAUMATIZED.

HE'S LUCKY, THOUGH— WE'RE ALL VERY SENSITIVE TO WHAT HE'S BEEN THROUGH..

..AND I'M SURE THE GUYS ARE GONNA DO WHAT THEY CAN TO HELP HIS NIGHT- MARISH MEMORIES FADE.

YEAH.

BOOF—GOT A MATCH?

SIR—THINK BACK, OKAY? THIS MORNING, WHEN OUR ATTACK ON THE GREEN SHIP WAS REPELLED?

AND WE WERE ALL SCRAMBLING TO GET BACK IN THE ROWBOAT, KICKING AND CRAWLING OVER EACH OTHER..

..DODGING THEIR BULLETS AND SCREAMING, "I DON'T WANNA DIE, I DON'T WANNA DIE"?

YEAH?

DID I HAVE MY THERMOS?

HEY—REMEMBER A COUPLE WEEKS AGO WHEN I STOLE YOUR "BEST CROW'S NEST GUY" TROPHY AND THREW IT IN THE HOLD WHERE ALL THE SLUDGE COLLECTS?

YEAH?

WELL, IT'S TAKEN ME AWHILE BUT I'VE FINALLY FORGIVEN MYSELF AND I'M READY TO PUT IT ALL IN THE PAST.

HEY—DO I IGNORE YOUR SMALL PERSONAL TRIUMPHS?

ANYTHING ELSE I SHOULD TELL THE GUYS BEFORE THE BATTLE, SIR?

YEAH, SEAHAWK..

COULD EVERYBODY PLEASE TRY NOT TO DIE ON THE NEW CARPETING?

HAVE YOU EVEN CRACKED THAT BOOK I GAVE YOU ON PEOPLE SKILLS?

YOU SEEM TALLER SINCE THE BATTLE.

WHAT DO YOU MEAN, "TALLER"?

I DON'T KNOW..

..TALLER.

CHARLEY, WOULD YOU PLEASE HAND ME THAT ROPE?

I'D BE HAPPY TO, SEAHAWK..

AND THEN LATER ON MAYBE YOU CAN HELP ME WITH THESE GOSH-AWFUL HEAVY BARRELS.

I'D LOVE TO..

AND MEANWHILE, ISN'T IT JUST A LOVELY, LOVELY AFTERNOON?

WHADDYA GOT THE GUYS DOING, NATE?

PRACTICING FOR PARENT'S DAY.

SIR, YOU KNOW THAT COURSE YOU CHARTED ON THE MAP TO SAIL US SOUTH TO SOME NICE, WARM ISLANDS?

YEAH?

AND I SAID, "LET'S DOUBLE-CHECK IT," BUT YOU SAID, "TRUST ME, NATE, OUR NEXT STOP IS JAMAICA"?

YEAH?

COME HERE A SECOND.

HAVE YOU TOLD THE GUYS THAT YOU ACCIDENTALLY SAILED US WAY, WAY NORTH INSTEAD OF SOUTH TO JAMAICA?

YEAH, SEAHAWK AND CHARLEY KNOW..

OBVIOUSLY, THEY WERE EXTREMELY BUMMED OUT. NOW I'M GONNA GO TALK TO BOOF..

ALTHOUGH BY NOW I DON'T KNOW WHAT I CAN TELL HIM HE DOESN'T ALREADY KNOW JUST BY LOOKING AROUND.

.. and get this, Mom — Jamaica has polar bears!!

WHAT A GREAT BUNCH OF PIRATES I HAVE, NATE. I LOCK US INTO AN ICE FIELD AND WE'RE PROBABLY DOOMED, RIGHT?

BUT DO THEY BLAME ME? NO — I SAIL 'EM INTO WHAT AMOUNTS TO CERTAIN DEATH, AND THIS FANTASTIC BUNCH OF GUYS DOESN'T EVEN BLAME ME.

HI, SIR—THANKS FOR KILLING US.

WELL, OKAY, MAYBE THEY BLAME ME A LITTLE..

TRY IT AGAIN.

BOO.

LOUDER, MAYBE.

BOO!

YOU SURE ABOUT THIS? HEY, RIGHT HERE: "'Yeti,' or 'Abominable snowman,' shy creature who inhabits snowy regions of the north..

..frightens easily."

HEY, COME ON, SIR— DON'T FEEL BAD ABOUT SAILING US TOO FAR NORTH AND GETTING US STUCK IN THE ICE.

WE'RE A TOUGH, DISCIPLINED CREW. WE WON'T LOSE HOPE, AND WE'LL SURVIVE THIS ORDEAL NO MATTER HOW LONG IT TAKES, OKAY?

THANKS, BOOF.

SO WHADDYA GOT THERE?

OH, JUST THE OFFICE POOL ON WHEN WE RESORT TO CANNIBALISM.

BOOF— WE'RE HURRYING TO GET HELP FOR OUR ICE-BOUND SHIPMATES, RIGHT?

THEY HAVE NO FOOD, NO WATER, AND THEIR ONLY HOPE IS IF WE GET BACK THERE WITH HELP FAST.

SO I KNOW IT'S AT THE RISK OF SOUNDING LIKE A REAL PARTY-POOPER HERE..

BUT COULD WE MAYBE STOP AND MAKE SNOW ANGELS LATER?

WE'RE GONNA MAKE IT, BOOF! WE'RE GETTING SO FAR SOUTH WE'RE OUT OF THE DANGEROUS ICE FIELD!!

YEAH!

FEELS GREAT TO BE GETTING BACK TO WHERE WE BELONG, HUH?

YUP—OUT OF THE ICE, OUT OF THE SNOW—

AND BACK TO THE COMFORT OF OUR NICE, SAFE..

..OCEAN.

ANYWAY, CAPTAIN DRUMMOND, IT WAS HEROIC OF YOU TO BREAK THROUGH THE ICE AND GIVE US THAT TOW.

YEAH.

YOU SAVED US FROM A HORRIBLE END, AND YOU HAVE CHARLEY AND SEAHAWK DUFFY'S GRATITUDE FOREVER AND EVER AND EVER.

DID YOU GET HIS WALLET?

CHARLEY, THE MAN JUST SAVED OUR LIVES—PLUS, HE HAD ONE OF THOSE LITTLE CHAINS ON IT..

WHAT ARE YOU DOING, BOOF?

WELL, I'M GETTING A REALLY BAD TOOTHACHE, CHARLEY, SO I'M TRYING TO BLOCK THE PAIN BY USING PLEASANT VISUAL IMAGERY.

COOL—IS IT WORKING?

YEAH, SO FAR..

CUZ I TRIED THAT ONCE AND ALL I COULD THINK OF WAS A TINY CRUEL SAVAGE IN MY MOUTH JABBING AT THE ROOT WITH A RED-HOT SPEAR.

WHO'S SCREAMING?

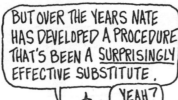

AS YOU KNOW, BOOF, WE DON'T HAVE ALL THE MODERN EQUIPMENT ON BOARD TO EXTRACT THAT BAD TOOTH OF YOURS..

BUT OVER THE YEARS NATE HAS DEVELOPED A PROCEDURE THAT'S BEEN A <u>SURPRISINGLY</u> EFFECTIVE SUBSTITUTE.

YEAH?

THINK HE'D HAVE TIME TO TAKE <u>MINE</u> OUT?

WELL, YOU KNOW WHAT?

Dunham

I ALREADY ASKED HIM ABOUT IT..

I'M A LITTLE WORRIED ABOUT LETTING CHARLEY AND SEAHAWK TAKE OUT BOOF'S BAD TOOTH.

YEAH?

BUT THEN AGAIN, IT'S NICE THAT THEY'RE ACTUALLY VOLUNTEERING TO HELP A SHIPMATE, RIGHT?

RIGHT.

AND WHO KNOWS? MAYBE FOR ONCE IN THEIR LIVES THEY'LL SURPRISE ME AND ACTUALLY USE A LITTLE JUDGMENT.

I'M GONNA HAVE TO TAKE ABOUT NINE OF THESE OUT JUST TO GET A LITTLE WORKING SPACE, CHARLEY.

WHATEVER DID WE LOAN OUT THE BIG POWER DRILL?

AS I TOLD THE CAPTAIN, BOOF— SEAHAWK AND I CAN PULL YOUR SORE TOOTH, BUT WE'RE NOT EXPERTS IN ANESTHESIOLOGY.

WHAT'S THAT, CHARLEY?

THAT'S PUTTING YOU UNDER FOR THE OPERATION. SO WE FARMED THAT OUT TO OUR COLLEAGUES IN THE CROW'S NEST.

GREAT—

SO WHEN DO WE START?

OH..

SOON..

ARE YOU STILL GONNA LET CHARLEY AND SEAHAWK PULL BOOF'S SORE TOOTH?

YEAH.

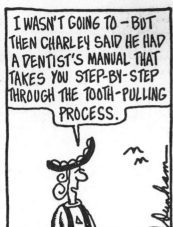

I WASN'T GOING TO — BUT THEN CHARLEY SAID HE HAD A DENTIST'S MANUAL THAT TAKES YOU STEP-BY-STEP THROUGH THE TOOTH-PULLING PROCESS.

SO I FIGURED, OKAY — THEY'RE RANK AMATEURS WITHOUT ANY TRAINING, BUT AT LEAST THEY'LL BE WORKING FROM A DECENT GUIDEBOOK.

"STEP ONE: IS THE BULL OR HEIFER HARNESSED AND HEAVILY SEDATED?"

SKIP AHEAD.

WAIT A MINUTE, CHARLEY — YOU GUYS WERE SUPPOSED TO PULL ONE OF BOOF'S TEETH AND YOU WOUND UP PULLING TWENTY-SIX OF 'EM?

YEAH.

DO YOU MIND IF I ASK WHY YOU DID THAT?

SEAHAWK KEPT DOUBLE-DOG DARING ME.

I THINK OUR LICENSE TO PRACTICE JUST GOT SUSPENDED.

DOES THAT AFFECT PAYMENT OF OUR BILL?

I WANT YOU TO KNOW, BOOF — CHARLEY AND SEAHAWK ARE GOING ON FULL REPORT FOR PULLING ALL YOUR TEETH.

THEY WERE SUPPOSED TO PULL ONE TOOTH — SO FOR THEIR TYPICAL MEANNESS THEY'RE GETTING FULL PUNISHMENT.

MAFFL BLIM TRNDLE FLOOFEN.

WELL, OKAY — HALF PUNISHMENT.

THEY DID FIX YOU UP WITH THE NICE SHARK DENTURES..